HORSES IN AMERICAN HISTORY

Norman D. Graubart

PowerKiDS press
New York

Published in 2015 by The Rosen Publishing Group, Inc.
29 East 21st Street, New York, NY 10010

First Edition

Editor: Amelie von Zumbusch
Photo Research: Katie Stryker
Book Design: Colleen Bialecki

Photo Credits: Cover Spencer Arnold/Stringer/Hulton Archive/Getty Images; p. 5 B. Speckart/Shutterstock.com; p. 6 OutdooRoar/iStock/Thinkstock; p. 7 smeola/Shutterstock.com; p. 8 Superstock/Getty Images; p. 9 MLADEN ANTONOV/Staff/AFP/Getty Images; p. 11 MPI/Stringer/Archive Photos/Getty Images; p. 12 De Agostini Picture Library/Getty Images; p. 13 (top) Archive Photos/Stringer/Getty Images; p. 13 (bottom) Joel St. Marie/iStock/Thinkstock; p. 14 Buyenlarge/Contributor/Archive Photos/Getty Images; p. 15 DEA Picture Library/Contributor/De Agostini/Getty Images; p. 16 Ron Embleton/The Bridgeman Art Library/Getty Images; p. 17 Apic/Contributor/Hulton Archive/Getty Images; p. 18 tfoxfoto/iStock/Thinkstock; p. 19 Diane Garcia/Shutterstock.com; p. 20 The Denver Public Library, Western History Collection; p. 21 Benalbright/iStock/Thinkstock; p. 22 Matthew D White/Photolibrary/Getty Images.

Library of Congress Cataloging-in-Publication Data

Graubart, Norman D.
Horses in American history / by Norman D. Graubart. — First edition.
pages cm. — (How animals shaped history)
Includes index.
ISBN 978-1-4777-6761-0 (library binding) — ISBN 978-1-4777-6762-7 (pbk.) —
ISBN 978-1-4777-6627-9 (6-pack)
1. Horses—United States—History—Juvenile literature. I. Title.
SF302.G6719 2015
636.1—dc23
2013046667

Manufactured in the United States of America

CPSIA Compliance Information: Batch #WS14PK5: For Further Information contact Rosen Publishing, New York, New York at 1-800-237-9932

CONTENTS

AMERICAN HORSES

What do the Denver Broncos football team and a Ford Mustang sports car have in common? Both of them have horses as their symbols. While horses have symbolized America and the Wild West for a long time, these animals actually came to America from Europe.

Many **breeds** of horses have been important in American history. Thoroughbreds are used in racing, while American Saddlebreds were widely used in the Civil War. Breeds such as the Kentucky Mountain horse and the quarter horse have been used for everything from farmwork to pleasure riding for hundreds of years.

Morgan horses are another American horse breed. All Morgan horses can be traced back to Figure, the horse that a New Englander named Justin Morgan bought in 1789.

ABOUT HORSES

Horses are large and sturdy animals. Smaller horses often weigh less than 1,000 pounds (454 kg), while large, heavy breeds can weigh more than 2,000 pounds (907 kg). Most breeds can carry a lot of weight, which has made them useful to humans for thousands of years. They also have flat backs, which makes it easy for humans to ride them.

Male horses are called stallions, while females are called mares. Young males are colts, while young females are fillies. Baby horses are called foals.

Arabians were bred in the deserts of the Middle East. These horses were bred to be used in wars. They are great long-distance runners and work well with people.

Horses were probably first used as work animals in the area that is modern-day Kazakhstan. This process is called **domestication**. Europeans and Asians helped create different breeds. Farmers, soldiers, and other people wanted horses for different reasons, so different breeds became good at different things.

EARLY AMERICA

There were many horse breeds in Colonial America. One of the first was the Narragansett Pacer. At the time, people were founding cities and settling the countryside. All kinds of people used these horses for riding long distances and hauling goods.

Riding horses tended to be the fastest way to get around, so important messages were often delivered on horseback. Here, a rider brings news of a key victory in the American Revolution.

Horses were important for travel. Early Americans rode horses and used them to pull carriages, as you can see in this photo of Colonial Williamsburg, a living-history museum in Virginia.

In the 1700s, settlers in Pennsylvania and Ohio developed the Conestoga horse. This was a draft horse, which means that it was used for farm or ranch work. These horses were used to pull Conestoga wagons, which were used to haul goods. Conestoga horses are now **extinct**. However, they were very important in the early days of American settlement.

NATIVE AMERICANS

You may have seen photographs and drawings of Native Americans on horses. However, these animals have been part of Native American **culture** only since the arrival of Europeans. Horses first came to the Americas with Spanish explorers in the early 1500s.

The arrival of horses in North America changed the way that many Native American tribes lived. Plains tribes began to use horses to hunt buffalo. Horses became a measure of wealth and status in many tribes. Many tribes also used horses in warfare, including in fights against the US Army as Americans moved west and began taking over native land.

This is a copy of a buffalo robe made by Native Americans to record a battle between the Pawnee and Kansa tribes in the early nineteenth century.

TIMELINE

1730

Bulle Rock becomes the first Thoroughbred brought to the American colonies.

1863

The Battle of Brandy Station takes place during the American Civil War. More than 18,000 **cavalrymen** fight in this battle.

1450 1500 1550 1600 1650 1700

1519

Spanish explorer Hernán Cortés lands in modern-day Mexico, bringing horses with him.

1919

A horse named Sir Belmont wins the Kentucky Derby, the Preakness Stakes, and the Belmont Stakes, becoming the first to win the horse racing Triple Crown.

1942

The last cavalry charge in American history takes place on January 16 in the Philippines against the Japanese army during World War II.

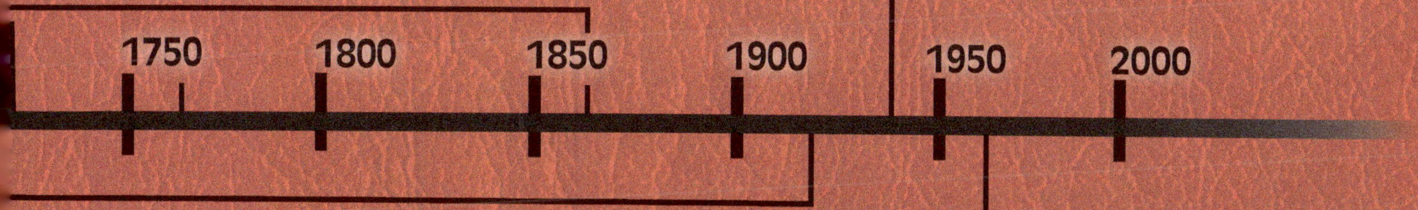

1959

Congress passes the Wild Horse Annie Act, which makes it illegal to hunt mustangs from the air or poison their water sources.

HORSES IN WAR

Horses have been used in battle for thousands of years. The military term for horse-riding soldiers is cavalry. American colonists used cavalry to fight the British during the American Revolution. One of the most famous battles involving cavalry was the Battle of Cowpens, in modern-day South Carolina. The colonists defeated the British in the battle.

In the Civil War, some horses carried officers and cavalrymen, while others pulled cannons, supplies, and ambulances. This print shows the Battle of Pea Ridge, which took place in Arkansas in 1862.

One of the conflicts between the Native Americans and the US Army in which horses played a key role was the Washita Massacre. It took place in Oklahoma in 1868.

In the Civil War, horses continued to be important. Confederate general Robert E. Lee rode a horse named Traveller. General Ulysses S. Grant of the Union rode one named Cincinnati. After the Civil War, Americans continued to move west. These settlers fought several battles on horseback with the Native Americans over land, including the Battle of the Little Bighorn.

HORSES IN THE WEST

Before trains were built in the nineteenth century, horses were the main means of **transportation**. Horses played a big part in the settlement of the West. Some of the first American settlers in the West kept cattle on large, open plains. Cowboys on horseback would round them up when the cows were old enough to be sold for their meat. Among a cowboy's most valued possessions were his horse and saddle.

Life in the West was hard, but horses made it a bit easier. They were used for transportation and in farming, ranching, mining, and the building of railroads.

This photograph of a cowboy was taken in Sturgis, South Dakota, around 1888.

Cowboys and their horses became famous symbols of the American West. Television shows featured characters such as the Lone Ranger, who was always riding his horse, Silver. Roy Rogers, another TV cowboy, rode Trigger.

A CHANGING ROLE

By the early twentieth century, trains were carrying Americans long distances. Cars replaced horse-drawn wagons for daily travel. Also, as the country grew, big farms began to replace small ones. This meant that big machines now did the farmwork that horses used to do.

The number of tractors on farms first passed the number of horses and mules in 1954. Today, most farms depend on machines like this one instead of horses.

Rodeos are a popular sporting event. Their roots can be traced back to the Spanish cattlemen who worked in what is now the American Southwest in the eighteenth century.

People still used horses, but they often did so in **leisure** activities, such as in horse racing. The Kentucky Derby has been run since 1875, and many other races have followed. Racehorses were, and still are, very expensive to buy. Some people own horses just because they think they are beautiful animals.

WILD HORSES

If there is a better symbol of the American West than the cowboy, it might be the mustang. Mustangs are **feral**. Feral animals are the wild **descendants** of domesticated animals. In the nineteenth century, there may have been as many as a few million mustangs roaming the West. By the middle of the 1900s, most of these horses had been hunted. Since then, **conservationists** have led efforts to protect wild mustangs.

Velma B. Johnston was known as Wild Horse Annie. She led a campaign to protect mustangs during the 1950s. The 1959 law that limited mustang hunting was named after her.

Chincoteague ponies live on Assateague Island, which is partly in Virginia and partly in Maryland. They are smaller, sturdier, and shaggier than most domesticated horses.

Today, there are about 32,000 mustangs in the West. There are also feral horse **populations** along the Atlantic coast, such as the Banker horses of North Carolina's Outer Banks and Chincoteague ponies in Virginia and Maryland.

HORSES TODAY

Horses are not as important to our daily lives as they used to be. However, some small farms still use horses instead of modern farm equipment to do farmwork.

Today, horses are most often used for riding. There are two main types of riding styles, Western and English. The Western style of riding is based on the way that cowboys used to ride horses in the American West. Horses will be part of American culture for many years to come!

Police officers still sometimes use horses. They use them to get around in remote areas and for crowd control in crowded ones.

GLOSSARY

breeds (BREEDZ) Groups of animals that look alike and have the same relatives.

cavalrymen (KA-vul-ree-men) The members of the part of an army that rides and fights on horseback.

conservationists (kon-ser-VAY-shun-ists) People who want to protect nature.

culture (KUL-chur) The beliefs, practices, and arts of a group of people.

descendants (dih-SEN-dents) Those that are born of a certain family or group.

domestication (duh-mes-tih-KAY-shun) Breeding or training animals to live with people.

extinct (ik-STINGKT) No longer existing.

feral (FER-al) Describing an animal that used to live with people but that has gone back to the wild.

leisure (LEE-zhur) Time to do whatever one wants.

populations (pop-yoo-LAY-shunz) Groups of animals or people living in the same place.

transportation (tranz-per-TAY-shun) A way of traveling from one place to another.

INDEX

WEBSITES

Due to the changing nature of Internet links, PowerKids Press has developed an online list of websites related to the subject of this book. This site is updated regularly. Please use this link to access the list:
www.powerkidslinks.com/anhi/horse/